# Riding With the Diaspora

Poems

John Palen

Author photo: Kent Curtis Miller
Cover art: © 2022 John Palen

ISBN: 979-8-9855242-1-5
Library of Congress Control Number: 2022930857

Sheila-Na-Gig Editions
Russell, KY
Hayley Mitchell Haugen, Editor
www.sheilanagigblog.com

# ACKNOWLEDGMENTS

I am grateful to the following publications where these poems originally appeared.

*Delmarva Review:* "At the Community Gardens," "Caches," "Digging Dandelions"

*Hamilton Stone Review:* "At the Supermarket After an Early Snow"

*Haunted Waters Press:* "Learning the Bones"

*Main Street Rag:* "Wearing the Shirts of Dead Men"

*Ocotillo Review:* Campbell's Tomato Soup"

*Off the Coast:* "Listening for Owls"

*Sheila-Na-Gig online:* "A Carefully Dressed Man," "The Back Shop," "How Things Change," "Pop. 546," "Pop. 2,422"

*Sleet:* "In the Pandemic, the Animals Return," "Learning to Float"

*The MacGuffin:* "Fall Equinox," "Freed Slave Cemetery, Texas," "North Branch, Chicago River"

*Willawaw Journal:* "Chicago Cold," "Cutting Button Blanks on the Illinois River," "His Gift," "Jack Pine," "Listening to the Katy Train," "Missouri Ozarks," "Riding With the Diaspora," "The Ridge at Meadowbrook"

I'm grateful also to poet friends Elaine Palencia, Judy Kerman, Emily Kerlin, Elizabeth Majerus, Gale Walden, Julie Price Pinkerton, Matt Murrey, Penelope Levine, Bob McDonough, Robert Manaster, Mary McCormack, Frank Modica, and Carol Sanford. You have encouraged me, laughed with me, and repeatedly saved me from my worst instincts.

And also to Hayley Haugen, who chose this manuscript as the winner of the 2021 Sheila-Na-Gig Editions poetry chapbook competition, and whose boundless energy, good sense and artistic vision brought this book to press.

# DEDICATION

To Ann, George, Emily, Caroline, Elinor and Dak.

And to Lois.

# CONTENTS

# The Ridge at Meadowbrook

Long before this was a city park curbed by busy streets,
playground and parking lot at one end,
herb garden and interpretive center at the other;
and before it was cropped land
with a farmhouse, windmill, barn and corncrib;
even before nomadic Kickapoo, those prodigious walkers,
ranged across it between Ontario and Mexico;
before all that, it was a windy glaciated ridge,
just beginning to birth wild prairie.

Even now, in winter, you can cross the ridgetop
on a paved path through prairie restoration
and feel that same wind, steady and cold,
that made the dry grasses bow to the ground
and rasp and moan to no one's hearing.
It blows right through you, that wind,
strips your thoughts and scatters them
as if you'd never been.

# Prairie Suite

1.

Prairie's a hairy beast,
humped brown shoulders
full of lice and ticks,
wet smelly sex tangle in her underparts.

Blowing snow, she doesn't give a damn,
spring makes her pretty, she doesn't
give a damn. I like to walk

in that indifference.

2.

Musk thistle mixed
with seed in a sack
or caught on a coat.
Wind catches a tuft

and away it goes
across Nebraska
to points west,

garlic mustard,
purple loosestrife,
smallpox, cholera
not far behind.

3.

We've parked our vans at the jumping-off places,
noses pointing west across the river
toward a sunset of gold.

Bug-spatters on the windshield
trouble the view, gray ghosts
of the Sac and Fox.

Here the Forty-Niners
dug a slope down the bank
to float wagons across

loaded with flour and hardtack,
beans, rice, coffee, tobacco,
a barrel of whisky

good as a tank of gas
and a credit card.

## Drawing Lines, 1842

The first surveyor of Holt County, Missouri,
finds honey in a tree but has nothing to carry it in.
An Indian woman, laughing, gives him a deer-skin pouch.
Days later, chopping a log, he gashes his leg with the axe.
An Indian man doctors him with chewed leaves,
stays with him three days until the fever breaks.

He admires the snug shelters of these Sac and Fox,
buffalo hides laid over poles and tied down.
He admires the way they teach children to stand early
by driving a long willow stick into the dirt
and giving the other end to the child to hold.

But when he watches one of them cut up a turkey,
strip the intestines clean between thumb and finger,
boil them and begin to eat —
(offering some to him, which he declines) —
he finds what he has been looking for all along,

and shrinks back within his whiteness. Days later,
laying out townships on the Indians' hunting grounds
with sextant and chain, he jots in his notebook:
"The blood in a man's veins counts for something, after all"

## Draining the Swamp

Before it was a cliché
for soft-handed politicians,
farmers in the Michigan Territory
did it with axe, spade and oxen
on hunting ground the Indians
"weren't doing a thing with."
The farmers prospered,
their cribs full most years,
their wives, children and stock
fed and housed. What they deemed
useless they got rid of —
bear, otter, cypress, whole
biomes. Kept their own dead
frozen in snow banks
until the sand ridges thawed
and they could dig the graves.
They worked their bodies hard.
The straight rows they plowed
still feed and impoverish us.

# The Morrow Plots

*University of Illinois, Urbana-Champaign*
*For James Treat*

This tenth-acre in a campus quad
on ditched and drained prairie
first sprouted corn the spring
Grant opened the Centennial Expo
and Custer went off hunting Sioux.
A cast-metal memorial says
it's what's left of "America's
oldest experimental field."

In today's blink of history's eye,
tassels stir in the breeze
behind a neatly clipped hedge.
Someone has written in cyberspace:
"I walked past these plots for years!
Much needed research and history!"
Another: "Sweet place to chill."
Another, in auto-translated Chinese:
"Running ran today. Good lawn."

But there's no plaque
for the Ancestral Puebloans of Mesa Verde,
those explorers who were cross-breeding maize
a couple thousand years ago
give or take. Mostly take.

# Freed Slave Cemetery, Texas

After seven years of drought
pulled back the lake's gray blanket,
photographers and gawkers
saw uncovered pine coffins,
forgotten tombstones, scattered bones.

Some limbs bore age deformities,
knitted lines from old fractures.
Others were straight, graceful,
as though these children might awaken
from a troubled sleep to appear

and testify about terrible crimes,
then tumble out among
bird song and dry grass
to breathe and play in the free air.

## Personal Effects

In a shoe box of newspaper clippings,
graduation announcements,
recital programs, letters from her sister,
memorabilia of a secure, contented life,

a crumbling brown document
from my mother's Virginia ancestors:
a bill of sale for a slave named Will —
a reminder of where I'm from.

# Listening to the Katy Train

The back yard was where my mother
hung laundry out to dry between two crosses,
her homesickness and our shabby house;
where my father nursed his weariness alone
and hid the empties under the trash.

Between our lot and the Katy tracks,
tangled, scabby apple trees went feral.
That was where I found nearsightedness,
squinting through an air rifle's notched iron,
the blurred distance closing in.

I was eleven that year Stalin died
in his own cramped quarters in the Kremlin.
Fixing supper, I heard the news on radio.
That night, beyond the ruined orchard,
the Katy train blared and rumbled out
to open country, shaking earth.

## The Way It Worked

Fathers told their sons
two things about sex: "Keep your
nose clean," whatever that meant,
and, "If some pervert lays
a hand on you I'll kill him."

So you knew, didn't you,
when I cut through the courthouse
and you pulled me into your office
and put my 12-year-old hand
on that ropy thing behind your fly
and asked, "Can you come yet, boy?"

and my reptilian brain spun me loose
and sent me scampering outside
into the sun stopped dead in the sky

you knew you could return to work
on the school truancy figures
safe in the knowledge
that I wouldn't tell

because I didn't want my father
to kill anyone.

## Boy on the Edge

Ten minutes to closing, he sprinkles
oily sawdust on the floor,
sweeps it down long aisles
with a bristle push broom.

Behind a curtain in the back
he scoops it into the trash.
The line of dirt left behind
he shoves into a dark corner.

It's there all night.
He's in trouble at home,
bored at school, hates his job.
The dirt nourishes his dreams.

# The Sleep of Gardeners

We didn't get along, Dad.
I wasn't your golden boy.
You weren't the father I needed,
the one I sought for years.

Trapped in your own problems
you didn't know how to help
when I dropped an easy fly
or a girlfriend dropped me.

I was mouthy. Once you struck me,
hard. I felt dizzy and sick for days.
You never hit me again.
I hope you were ashamed.

Yet when the frost goes out
I hoe furrows, like we did together,
plant seed, smell the breath
of wormy, crumbly soil

then sleep the delicious
long unbroken sleep
you taught me,
dreaming of plenty.

# Campbell's Tomato Soup

Long before it was a series of prints on canvas
that helped make Andy Warhol rich and famous

and long before it became something sneered at
by foodies and people who never cook at home

and long before it was renamed Classic
to distinguish it from the 18 other choices

including Disney Mickey Mouse, Healthy Request,
Harvest With Basil, and Parmesan Bisque,

it was something my mother served for lunch
with saltine crackers, peanut butter and milk

because it saved time for her, to open a can,
add water, heat it in a pan and pour,

no parsley garnish, no swirl of anything on top,
just plain hot soup in a bowl in a tiny kitchen

that looked out on a chicken coop, a vegetable garden,
an unpainted wooden gate where tramps left marks

to tell each other that if one came and asked
he would be fed. He would be fed.

# Self-Portraits

*LaSalle Street at Close of Day*
Alfred Juergens, 1915

From his 10th-floor studio he paints
skyscrapers at dusk
under smoke and low clouds,
warm light behind their windows
and down at the canyon's bottom
reflections on wet pavement,
streetcars lined up in the rain.

It's 27 years before I'm born
in a Missouri plains town
where everybody knew
everything about me
before I had a say in it.
Yet here I am in that multitude
of hurried people making way
around and through each other,
without a word or nod.

Maybe I'm the man holding
a soaked newspaper over his head.
Maybe I'm the news hawker
minding his stand. Maybe
I'm the boy who dodges
the mounted cop in a kepi,
blessed by anonymity,
destinations unknown.

## Pop. 2,422

The sharp smell of hot asphalt
at mid-day on the main drag,
diesel exhaust at the four-way,
the bar's wooden floor stale with spills.

No shade for a man in his own shadow,
no place to go, finally, but home.
All night the air conditioner
shudders on and off, on and off.

A slight breeze at dawn
stirs the catalpa grove,
a rustling of old violence
hushed for a hundred years.

## Pop. 5,717

*The team they play for*
*is famous in this town*
John Knoepfle

They are only boys,
long bones still growing,
brains still developing,
but tonight the white lights burn above the field,
chill autumn makes them horny
everywhere in their goose-bumped bodies
for the girls screaming in the stands,
and the band makes a racket in tribute to them
as if they were already heroes
though they are only boys.
And this is when their coaches
who are like their fathers tell them
"You can be as good at this as you want to be," and
"You need to want this, you need to want it,"
and "It's all up to you," then send them out
onto that green hundred yards of total, terrifying exposure
to hurt each other as much as they can.

# Pop. 546

Tracks cut the town in half:
two bars, a store and a church on one side,
shaded homes on the other. Elevators
that once rumbled with cascades of grain
stand empty now. Children play
red light, green light on an abandoned spur
where grass goes to seed in the rail bed.

There's no Interstate access.
The villagers have made peace with that.
Amtrak never runs on time,
freights pass through whenever,
blocking grade crossings at will.
"No clocks in the mountain monastery,"
says the man who keeps the produce stand,
a refugee gardener who washed up
here from Saigon in 1975.

## Missouri Ozarks

It's years since I've been back to this eroded tableland,
wooded peaks at the same elevation,
long climbs to the crests,
long descents to rivers that recite history,
Niangua, Big Piney, Gasconade.

Off the I-44, little towns like Buckhorn, Sleeper,
then farther into the hills, sporadic clusters
of two or three houses along winding roads,
unnamed places, not on a map.

I see a familiar house,
remember Albert, whose port wine stain
covered half his face, whose peonies,
petunias, sweet alyssum, begonias
were the neighbors' envy.

One night young men in a car plowed them up,
scattered dirty leaves and flowers in the yard,
the spinning tires such a small hatred
in such a small place.

# Learning the Bones

That was the summer I packed poetry in a box
and wrote obits. Hundreds, from little towns
like Neosho, Vinita and Siloam Springs.
I left Pound, Virgil and the New Criticism
arguing in the dark in a friend's basement
and wrote plain words about plain lives
in a sun-lit second-story newsroom
full of desks, ashtrays and phones.

The dead had dates, idiosyncratic names,
survivors who cared. No poem I've written
before or since has mattered as much.
I'd stay up late, poring over the day's work.
Accuracy, spelling, grammar, brevity:
That was the summer I learned the bones.

# Where We're From

When we're at loose ends we drive out into the country
to little towns like the ones we grew up in and fled:

a school, a few churches, one or two bars,
a grocery, grain elevator and farm supply.

We slow-drive the streets, admire tended yards
daubed orange with ditch lilies, purple with phlox,

dappled with shade from big oaks and maples.
"Idyllic-looking little place," one of us will say,

"look at that nice old Victorian." And the other:
"We could buy a lovely house here cheap."

"Yeah, and do what?" "Go crazy in a year and leave."
It's patter, a routine to gloss over memories

of a sundown town, a superintendent who molested boys,
a Scout troop that trashed a paraplegic's corner store.

Still, people cared for us, taught us math, drafting,
independence. They were happy for us when we left.

Conflicted, grounded again, we take a fraying street out of town,
follow the dashboard compass through tall green fields

on nameless, back-country oil-and-chip roads
that jog every mile or so toward home.

# Love

*After Erich Fried*

I don't know what it is, really,
but maybe
it's something like this:

When we go to hear
the university orchestra
and they're playing
Bartok's *Concerto for Orchestra*
which is over their heads
and which they will probably
perform only this once in their lives

and they arrive
at that great fugal passage
in the fifth movement
and against all odds
leap hurdles
like thoroughbreds and
by God!
make music

and we turn to each other
at the same moment
grins spreading
across our faces —

maybe that's love
or something close enough.

# North Branch, Chicago River

*Halsted Street Bridge*
James Bolivar Needham, 1918

Crossings brought me here:
one from Africa, generations ago;
one that my parents undertook
on the Underground Railroad

to slave-haven Chatham, Ontario;
my own as a deckhand on the lakes,
learning to see water as an artist,
teaching my hand to paint.

At the Columbian Exposition,
I was hired help on the murals.
That's how I came to be
a Black artist in the White City.

    \* \* \*

Chicago roars upward, reaches high,
rebuilding in steel after the Great Fire.
I like to paint this low, quiet place
where the inferno drew up just short

of old wooden buildings
at the tip of Goose Island,
where only pine masts scrape the sky
above orange and green hulls.

A lift bridge with double arches
keeps passages open —
up and down the river,
across the city, across time.

I'm like the bridgetender
whose tiny red-roofed house
I daubed in at one end of the span:
I keep an eye out.

# Cutting Button Blanks on the Illinois River

It was long hours in riverside sheds,
the line shaft's rumble and snap,
the drill bit's whine,
the wet clatter of shell in waste piles
like ice falling from a roof.

It was bread and coffee
until he learned the craft
and no longer got docked;
then it was salt pork and beans.
It was drinking pain away
Saturday nights in Peoria.

There was art to it:
Elktoe mussels took the drill
a certain way, Wartybacks another.
He had to sense his way into the work
with fingers raw from wet sand
and rough shell.

When zippers and plastic came in,
the river harvesters sold off
their crowfoot hooks for scrap.
No one knows anymore
how to drill button blanks
or shape and polish them.

Old, depleted as the mussel beds,
he keeps mother-of-pearl
buttons in a box,
takes them out sometimes
to hold luster in his hand.

# The Back Shop

Deep in the back of the building,
far from Uncle Ralph's genteel office
with its revises and flimsies,
Uncle Pete had his domain,
hot as a foundry, busy as hell.
Wheeled iron turtles,
chases, quoins and a hellbox.
The Linotype's metallic clatter,
smells of gasoline and cigarettes,
oil and grit on every surface,
a thinning oval of Lava soap
on a basin stained with ink and rust.

He sends me to the alley for lead pigs,
two-foot gray bars in a pile
among tall dandelions.
From a hooked chain they'll feed
a melting pot at 700 Fahrenheit,
hot enough to explode
if he spills his Coke.

Deadline nears.
His quick two-fingered jabs
add substance and weight to words
by casting them into type.

# Jack Pine

*Squally Weather, Georgian Bay*
F. H. Varley, 1920

They call me the unlucky tree,
say I poison soil, make women barren,
sicken grazing cattle. Those are lies.
I'm a twisted, stocky runt,
but good in the hard going.

This is my kind of weather,
north wind pushing whitecaps
under a choppy, bruised-ochre sky.
Feet fixed in the Canadian Shield,
I dance waving my arms.

I hang on to my tight cones,
wait for wildfire to free the seeds.
They find burnt ground, acid bog,
thin soil in granite hollows.
I dig in. I make it work.

# Lost Brothers

*Hurdy Gurdy*
Lawren Harris, 1913

I remember the birches spilling
yellow-gold that day
on the narrow row houses
of Toronto's immigrant ward.

I was the girl in a red coat
in a corner of the painting,
giving the organ grinder's boy
a penny or maybe a bun.

My two brothers,
daubed-in figures beside me,
waited. They would die in war.
I wish now I could see their faces.

Some people paid the organ grinder
to scram, go somewhere else
to play her only tune.
But in that golden light

I liked it, wanted it to go on,
the notes drifting up
into the yellow leaves,
the leaves drifting down.

# Chicago Cold

*Red House and Elevated Train*
Francis Chapin, early 1930s

It's primeval, starts in the polar vortex,
nothing in its way until it reaches you
walking home through North Town
from Sedgewick Station in a cheap coat,

a damp, stiff wind at your hunched back.
You never knew cold until salty slush
wicked to your feet through leaky shoes
and thin socks. Never knew cold

until a gust straight out of South Dakota
buffeted the L, swerved and came for you
and your porkpie hat. Never knew how cold

until you came to this red brick four-flat
with a jet of snow streaming off the cornice
a long block from home.

# Window Tables in the Loop

Walking past, I see them in pairs
behind etched glass in pricey restaurants,
matrons in black pantsuits,
pale blouses and peacock scarves,
with perfect eyebrows in copper bas relief.

They eat deliberately, a salad,
nodding and smiling at each other
but not at us, never a glance
though they know we're there,
tourists, gawkers who know nothing
about carrying the weight of Chicago.

I imagine them as high-cheeked girls
growing up in the Polish Triangle,
married early to big men
who shouldered their way through life
until they were seized by their own hearts
and wrestled to the ground.

The widows reserve these window tables
(they have earned every fine touch)
so they can be seen and admired. And I do.

# At the Supermarket After an Early Snow

Winter blew through like a rude guest,
didn't stay, left old socks on the berm.
It will be back in dirty moraines,
ice in dangerous ridges underfoot.

While geese stage in the stubble fields,
snowbirds pack for the Rapture
to be whisked away to Florida.
I'll winter in place, as I've always done,

with the man from the group home
in damp parka and yellow safety vest
who'll pilot nested carts across the parking lot
like lake freighters in a November gale;

with the frail greeter on a tripod cane
who'll welcome shoppers at gray dawn
at a door always opening to the cold.

## Sweet Chariot

In a corner of a bus-stop shelter
an old bent woman with a perm
in shorts and thin shirt in chilly autumn
stoops among trash and blown leaves.

She sweeps them up with her fingers,
bins them, clears a tidy space.
When she finds a usable butt
she blows ash and dirt off it

rises up and takes two steps
to her belongings on a cold stone bench.
She saves the butt among her things
and bends to work again.

A lumbering bus swings round the corner,
rolls to a stop, and kneels.

# After a Funeral, Soccer in the Street

He and his parents made it out
in '38. Others in the family didn't.
Word came slowly, if at all.

He was quick to argue,
quick to anger. Shouted like Stentor,
with the voice of fifty men.
Knew operas by heart. Rose early,
always first on the slopes.

I saw him toward the end, rapt,
*Die Zauberflöte* playing across his face
in a dark cinema,
head held straight and still.
Parkinson's had thinned the voice
to a whisper, taken away
the ski legs, revealed
a different man.

At the funeral a daughter spoke:
*Who would have thought my father*
*would have handled this with such grace?*

That afternoon his children
and their children and partners and spouses,
those he loved and yelled at,
played soccer in the street
in shirt sleeves in the December light,

two sexes, three genders, four languages,
swooping and crossing each others' arcs
like swallows in flight.

# In the Pandemic, the Animals Return

Shut inside, we see them
flowing back into our lives
like tide reclaiming a shallow bay.

Across our television screens,
fish flash in the clear canals of Venice,
boars wander a Barcelona eight-lane,
coyotes trot grandly through the Loop.
We have time now to observe
male flickers doing their shy, funny
challenge dances at our windows.

The man waking from a long coma
sees animals in the corner of his eye.
Foxes and cats and shadows
sit quietly in the room.
They watch over him.

# How Things Change

The neglected dam at Edenville
holds back eighty million tons of water,

generates a little power for the grid,
a little worry for the powers that be.

Then weeks of rain, until the watershed
has had it, can't hold any more.

The lake overtops the spillway,
liquifies embankments. The dam fails,

the flood tumbles, ranging free
through low woodlands, streets, houses,

rising, rising, rising. Nothing can stop it
until it's satisfied. And even if you live

downstream and have much to lose,
that part of you still capable of awe

will say, Let it come. Let it come.

## Listening for Owls

Winter night, snow on the ground,
bare trees under a whetted moon.
The trail steward plays a tape
of the barred owl's questioning:
Who cooks for you? Who cooks for you?
In answer, a distant trill, just one,
faint as a chirp on a cellphone.
That's all. Not what we wanted.

"What else do you hear?" she whispers.
We shake our heads. Nothing.
But children breathe, quiet and steady,
and boots shift in snow.
"An owl would hear that," she says,
"anywhere in the woods."

## Cooper's Hawk

I spend a lot of time waiting,
perfectly still, high in a tree,
upright and brown as bark.

You'll stare, try to decide
if I'm bird or branch,
but you'll tire and look away,
and then I'll move my head
with a quick, exact turn.

In flight I maneuver well,
swoop low, dodge obstacles
in forest or prairie grove.
I'll surprise you, mouse,
just as you hear my wings.

# Digging Dandelions

He can hardly swallow, needs help
with intimate functions,
yet here he is, sitting in grass
digging dandelions.

He knows the yard's a seed bank
of weeds, knows new bursts
of yellow will dot the lawn
next spring when he'll be dead.

Digs anyway. When his long
body starts to pivot at the hips,
ticks down like a second hand,

the caregiver catches him
in time, gently tips him
up again to twelve.

# Caches

Squirrels bury their surplus
in a thousand places, nuts and seeds
they have to find again to survive.
I always admired your knack for detail,
how you could shape a tooth,
fly a twin-engine plane, make oboe reeds,
tens of thousands over a lifetime.
Now you fumble pajama buttons,
take two hours to dress, can't say
what lies ahead, if anything,
in the mind's foggy, wintry day.
Outside your patio door, a squirrel
noses snow-crusted dirt,
here, here and here; it must be deft
with Cooper's Hawks around.
After lunch, you take the oboe from its case,
choose a reed, run graceful scales.

Your fingers know the keys.

# At the Community Gardens

The crew at the senility wing next door
keeps busy making connections,
nailing studs to plates, ceiling joists
to rafters. Today's news was Trump, Covid,
a homeless man in a wheelchair
riding buses back and forth across L.A.
I squat in my rain-soaked garden,
pulling bindweed out of the onions.

I used to think gardening would help
save the world. Such a peaceable thing,
you and I and the next person
and the next, like kids donating dimes
or cleaning their plates. Now I think
it has only helped me reach old age.

The rough, wet tongues of crabgrass
lick my muddy hands. When I stand up
the air darkens, daylight drains.
I spook the sparrows. As old
as I in sparrow years, they explode
out of the roofers' scrap pile
like hard, quick heartbeats
and vanish into the trees.

# The Problem With Shoes

One foot is always larger.
Clerks tell you, put on both shoes,
walk around. Then they stretch
the tight one on a wooden tool
resembling a lobster claw.
Your shoes feel good in the store
but after you get them home
they change, and your feet
change in that dark intimacy.
Finally one shoe or the other
will pinch or chafe
until the pair is broken in.
Then they're great,
so comfortable, almost perfect,
though you notice
they're beginning to wear
a little each day, like friends
you've grown old with and come to love
though you see their flaws so clearly,
the awful things they've done,
what it means to be broken in.

# Wearing the Shirts of Dead Men

A man's wife buys him a shirt for his last weeks.
He wears it only once, sitting up at home, listening to music.
A man buys a shirt, has a heart attack or a massive stroke.
A man buys a shirt for a business trip to California.
His plane crashes on takeoff. The shirt, in misdirected luggage,
waits for days in a small, dark room.

Shirts that lie in drawers for six months, a year,
some still folded and pinned, tissue and cardboard intact.
Finally they go to resale. I spot them on the rack, crisp and colorful
among the softer faded ones. On each cuff
two buttons, another halfway up the sleeve placket.
Snug button holes. Earth tones, maroon-and-gray checks.

All these dead men. I come across their shirts, like new.
I buy them for a song.

# Fall Equinox

*Horse and Train*
Alex Colville, 1954

As we turn toward darkness,
look at this black horse
racing headlong down the tracks,
hooves pounding ballast and ties.

Its huge rump propels a half ton
of muscle, bone, blood, organs, nerves
into the future, where a black train
rounds the bend, takes aim.

The headlight catches the rails.
Heavy pistons pound like hooves,
smoke billows over the twilit prairie.
Surely the train will brake, the horse veer.

But no. The machine was made to overpower,
the horse is steeled to meet it head-on.
There's only this opposition,
and the gleaming rails.

# A Carefully Dressed Man

*Self-Portrait*
Edward Hopper, 1925-1930

He is turned partway toward us,
this man in a soft brown fedora,
comfortable gray jacket, green tie,
blue shirt with upturned collar tips.

At his back, a blank wall,
plain baseboard at the floor line,
an unopened door in cove framing.
Is he going out? And where?

Under the wide brim's shadow,
light falls on neck and cheek,
the fleshy mouth. In the eyes,
something vulnerable and elusive,

the way they half observe us,
half look away. Is it our
gaze he shies from, or his own?

## Old Man With a Gold Chain

*Rembrandt van Rijn, c. 1631*
*Art Institute of Chicago*

You're getting old, too, you know.
I've watched you
since you started coming here
on Sundays on the Metra, jammed in
with Bears fans and the obnoxious young.
At first you kept your distance,
circling the gallery,
grazing the Old Masters while you
read all the labels. Lately
your gait has slowed, you can't stand as long.
You look more, read less. You spend
more time with me, up close.

I've examined you, as well.
You've lost height and weight, shrunk
in clothes that once showed your importance.
Your neck's gotten scrawny.
You neglect yourself,
don't shave as carefully,
leave long white hairs around the Adam's apple.
I see small folds the color of chicken skin
around your thousand-yard stare.
You'll die like me,
a monumental wreck of a man.

# Learning to Float

*For Dale Trinka, Edwardsville YMCA*

Boys twice my age tossed me into the deep end.
I was five. The sunlit chop flashed blue and gold
as I sank, gulped water, struggled up and sank again.

Somehow I reached the gutter, pulled myself up
into their laughter. I wondered why nobody cared.
Deep in my brain, the little amygdala wondered, too.

In my early middle age you taught me to float:
Lie back, you said. Relax, keep your butt up.
No matter how deep the water is, you'll be okay.

And I became a fanatic, a born-again swimmer,
learning all the strokes, doing laps every day,
even holidays if I could find an open pool,

until I kicked that, too, and at last floated free.

# His Gift

All winter the tools hung in neat rows
in her cold garage:
saws, screwdrivers, try squares,
among them her father's old hammer,
the handle spattered with paint,
the head so rusty
she doesn't use it anymore.

He had a temper, and she was frightened of him,
but she liked to go out to his wood shop
in the machine shed next to the barn,
watch him build simple furniture,
and hand him screws and washers
from rows of dusty jars.

Spring has come, her garage has warmed,
she's cutting half-laps and mortises.
She's forgotten about the flaws
in last year's projects,
and when it's time for lunch
she leaves everything where it is
so she can pick up where she left off.

A marking tool, a mallet and three chisels
face every-which-way in the curled shavings
like five horses grazing in a windless pasture.

## St. O'Hare Cathedral

Not enough snow to bother a Chicago cabbie,
but enough to jam the airport with delays
that cascade nationwide. Hope for a flight home
coughs and flames out. I'm rebooked
for 6 a.m., the hotels are full,
so I eat a stale Danish, spread my coat
on a three-seat bench
and try to sleep.

Hours later
I'm rolling in the stagnant pond of self
like a dying carp. If I drift off,
the seat divider under my hip
goads me awake again.

And then I sleep.

And then I wake to perfect stillness,
watery blue light flowing in
through tall clear windows
under an arched ceiling.

And into that high silence
a janitor pushes a wide mop
and sings quietly to himself,
a blues, a hymn.

# Riding With the Diaspora

The air is sharp with the sound of Chinese, sweet with Spanish,
like a good sauce, and everyone is going home,
but not really; home on the bus to small apartments
but not *home* home, not Guangzhou or Saltillo,
Chongquing or Cartagena.

At 6:00 on a winter evening
we're all diaspora, all a little homesick.

If you weren't on the bus, you missed
the Chinese father and his toddler
who boarded at the day-care stop
with Italian takeout in a clamshell,
its good, garlicky smell
available for everyone to share.

You missed the way he lifted her
onto the quickly vacated bench seat
and the way her dark eyes
stared at our human faces.

# ABOUT THE AUTHOR

Life-long Midwesterner John Palen worked as a store clerk, draftsman, newspaper reporter, editor, and journalism teacher. Over the last 50 years his poems have appeared in such publications as *Poetry Northwest, Sou'wester, Birmingham Poetry Review,* and *The Formalist,* and in anthologies published by Wayne State University Press and Milkweed Editions. He won the *Passages North* Poetry Competition in 1989 and has been a Pushcart and Best of the Net nominee. He earned a doctorate in American Studies at Michigan State University and was awarded a National Endowment for the Humanities journalism fellowship at Johns Hopkins University. Mayapple Press brought out *Open Communion: New and Selected Poems* in 1994 and *Distant Music* in 2017. Recent work has appeared in *Cider Press Review, Sleet, The MacGuffin, Willawaw Journal, Sheila-Na-Gig online, Off the Coast, Great Lakes Review,* and *Delmarva Review.* He lives, writes and gardens on the Illinois Grand Prairie.